WE BELIEVE IN THE ONE TRUE AND LIVING GOD.
HE IS THE CREATOR AND SUSTAINER OF THE UNIVERSE, WHO IS ALL-WISE,
ALL-POWERFUL. HE IS RULER OVER EVERYTHING AND DIRECTS THE
ACCORDING TO HIS ETERNAL PURPOSES.
(GENESIS 1:1-3, ISAIAH 44:6, 24, ISAIAH 45:5-7, MARK 12:29-32, ACTS 17:25B-28).

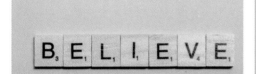

WE BELIEVE THAT JESUS CHRIST IS GOD'S BELOVED SON. BEING IN VERY NATURE GOD, HE WAS PRESENT AND ACTIVE IN CREATION. HE LIVED ON THIS EARTH, TAUGHT MEN TO KNOW THE PATH TO SALVATION, AND WAS CRUCIFIED FOR OUR SINS TO RECONCILE US WITH GOD. HE WAS RAISED FROM THE GRAVE ON THE THIRD DAY AND ASCENDED INTO HEAVEN TO SIT AT THE RIGHT HAND OF GOD, WHERE HE NOW INTERCEDES WITH THE FATHER ON OUR BEHALF. WE BELIEVE IN HIS EVENTUAL RETURN, HIS ULTIMATE VICTORY OVER SATAN, AND HIS ETERNAL REIGN.
(MATTHEW 28:2-7, JOHN 1:1-3, JOHN 3:16, JOHN 14:6, ROMANS 8:34, EPHESIANS 1:18-23, PHILIPPIANS 2:6, COLOSSIANS 1:17-20, 2 PETER 1:11, REVELATION 12:10-11).

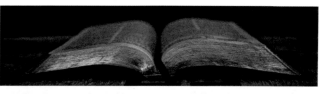

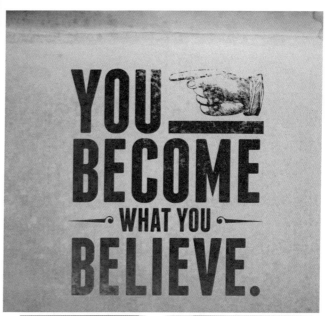

Support

GUIDANCE
ENCOURAGEMENT

WE BELIEVE IN THE HOLY SPIRIT.

HE IS ONE WITH THE FATHER AND SON AND LIVES WITHIN THE CHURCH, INDIVIDUALLY AND COLLECTIVELY DIRECTING OUR MINDS, GIVING US LIFE, EMPOWERING US TO CONFESS THAT JESUS IS LORD, TESTIFYING THAT WE ARE GOD'S CHILDREN, AND INTERCEDING FOR US IN OUR PRAYERS
. (JOHN 14:6, ROMANS 8:5-17; 26-27, I CORINTHIANS 3:16; 6:19; 12:3).

ETERNAL LIGHT

#GOD
IS
LOVE

Easter

LENT
Fasting
Praying
Almsgiving

HAPPY EASTER

HAPPY EASTER

holy week

JESUS

WE BELIEVE THAT SALVATION COMES ONLY THROUGH JESUS CHRIST.
ALL OF US HAVE SINNED, AND OUR SIN SEPARATES US FROM THE HOLY GOD. HOWEVER, WE ARE
RECONCILED TO GOD THROUGH CHRIST'S SACRIFICE FOR US, CAUSING OUR HEARTS TO REPENT
OF OUR FORMER SINFUL WAYS, CONFESS BEFORE MEN THAT JESUS IS LORD, AND CARRY OUT OUR
OBEDIENCE IN BAPTISM (IMMERSION). WE HAVE RAISED FROM THE WATER A NEW CREATURE,
DESIGNED TO CARRY OUT THE WORKS OF SERVICE GOD HAS RESERVED FOR EACH OF US AND TO
GROW TOWARD THE CHRISTLIKE CHARACTER THAT HE DESIRES.
(MATTHEW 10:32-33, MARK 16:16, JOHN 10:9, ACTS 2:38, ACTS 4:12, ACTS 26:20B, ROMANS, 3:23, ROMANS
4:6-8, ROMANS 5:11, 11 CORINTHIANS 5:18-21, EPHESIANS 2:10, EPHESIANS 5:2, COLOSSIANS 1:22-23A).

BIBLE
STUDY

WE BELIEVE THAT THE BIBLE IS THE INSPIRED WRITTEN WORD OF GOD. THROUGH THE BIBLE, GOD REVEALS HIS HOLY NATURE AND THE DESIRE FOR A COVENANT RELATIONSHIP WITH HIS CHILDREN. THE BIBLE IS THE COMPREHENSIVE AND AUTHORITATIVE GUIDE TO RIGHT LIVING AND CHRISTIAN CONDUCT AND OUTLINES GOD'S PLAN TO RECONCILE ALL MEN TO HIMSELF THROUGH JESUS CHRIST. (PSALM 19:7-11, PROVERBS 30:5-6, PHILIPPIANS 1:27, 2 TIMOTHY 3:16).

CREATOR

PARADISE

HEAVEN

Goddess

I am Worthy

GOD

mercy

THE LORD WHO PROVIDES

WE BELIEVE JESUS CHRIST ESTABLISHED HIS CHURCH.
HIS DESIRE IS FOR A UNIFIED COMMUNITY OF FOLLOWERS, WHO ACT AS HIS
AMBASSADORS TO CARRY THE GOOD NEWS OF SALVATION TO ALL MEN, AND SERVE
OTHERS IN HIS NAME. THE CHURCH ENCOURAGES EACH OTHER AND ASSEMBLES TO
WORSHIP JESUS OUR RISEN LORD AND GOD THE FATHER.
(MATTHEW 28:19-20, ACTS 2:41-47, EPHESIANS 2:19-22, EPHESIANS 3:10, HEBREWS 10:24-25).

WE BELIEVE THAT JESUS CHRIST WILL RETURN.
A JUDGMENT OF ALL MEN'S ACTIONS AND INTENTS WILL TAKE PLACE, AND THOSE WHO HAVE FAITHFULLY SERVED JESUS WILL, THROUGH HIS GRACE AND MERCY, LIVE WITH HIM FOR ALL ETERNITY IN HEAVEN.
(MATTHEW 16:17, JOHN 14:1-3, 2 CORINTHIANS 5:10, PHILIPPIANS 3:20, I PETER 1:3-5).

GOD MY ROCK

SALVATION

BLESSING

PEACE in the WORLD

Grace

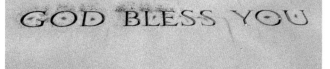

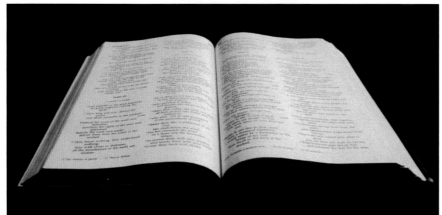

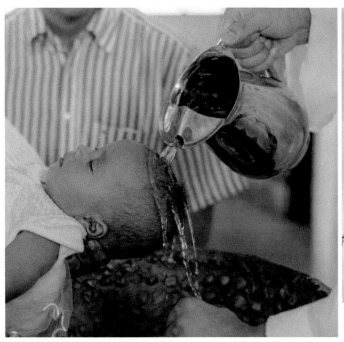

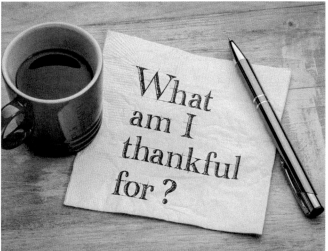

I am with you.
-God

PSALM 107

O GIVE thanks unto the LORD, for he is good: for his mercy endureth for ever.
2 Let the redeemed of the

GOD LOVES ME

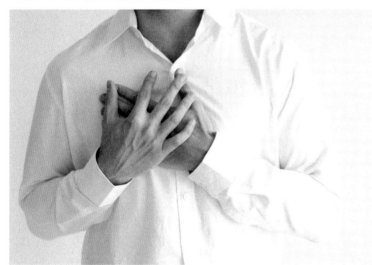

the greatest entity in existence

SUPREME BEING

ETERNAL

LIFE

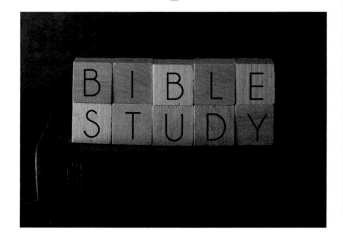

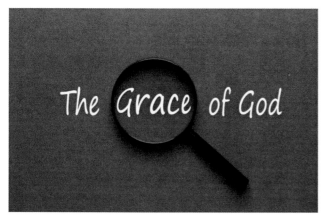

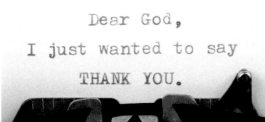

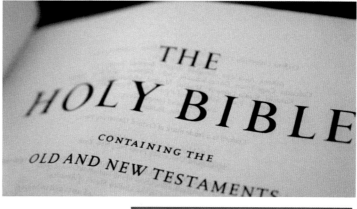

CONVICTION

ACCEPTANCE

LOVE

FAMILY

HUG

CONFIDENCE

Loyalty

TRUTH

GOOD HEALTH

GOOD FOOD

GOOD TIME

ABUNDANCE
GRATEFUL

wisdom

KINDNESS

DEV♥TION

JOY

Thank you

for choosing our
Vision Board
Clip Art Book

As a special GIFT
I am offering you a
complimentary guide to
download.

This guide is designed to help
you confidently create your
vision board, set SMART
goals, and embrace unlimited
possibilities for your dreams.

Open the camera on your phone
(as if you're going to take a photo)
Hold the phone on the QR CODE below then
a link will appear on your screen
Tap on the link to get your FREE GUIDE

FREE GUIDE

Your Guide to
Creating the Life You
Dream Of

*designed to help you clarify your values, align your beliefs, and set
actionable, meaningful goals that reflect your true self*

Leen W.Hart

Much Love
Leen

Made in the USA
Las Vegas, NV
06 January 2025